MEMORY LANE
BARROW

MEMORY LANE BARROW

NORTH-WEST
Evening Mail

breedon **books**
PUBLISHING

First published in Great Britain in 2001 by
The Breedon Books Publishing Company Limited
Breedon House, 3 The Parker Centre, Derby, DE21 4SZ.

ISBN 1 85983 240 7

Printed and bound by Butler & Tanner, Frome, Somerset
Jacket printing by GreenShires Ltd, Leicester

Contents

Foreword

BARROW has grown used to change. New ways of working, new lifestyles, new ways to travel and new forms of leisure.

The effects of those changes can be clearly seen as you turn the pages of *Memory Lane Barrow*.

Barrow was born in the middle of the great Victorian industrial age and proved to be a strong child.

From a few farms and fishermen's cottages, Barrow was transformed into a busy port and became the hub of a new railway network needed to meet the insatiable demand for the iron ore riches found deep underground in the mines of Furness.

The new town grew at breakneck speed, drawing families from all corners of the British Isles. Its key industries of iron and steel, engineering and shipbuilding became world leaders.

Memory Lane Barrow draws its pictures from the last 60 years – a period of major and sometimes painful adjustment to the needs and ways of the modern world.

Who could have imagined that the mighty iron and steel industry, which once employed thousands of workers, would be no more than a memory?

You can gauge the age of a Barrovians by how many town centre redevelopments they have lived through.

The latest one we feature swept away Forshaw Street. Before that it was the likes of Paxton Street, the old market and shops around Cavendish Square which had a date with the bulldozers.

Other well-loved victims of demolition are recorded, such as Her Majesty's Theatre, the Coliseum, Walney Cinema and the Electric Cinema.

Earlier still was the Barrow Blitz of 1941 – an unwanted but not unexpected consequence of being a vital naval shipbuilder during World War Two.

For those not old enough to have been there, it is hard to appreciate how much damage it caused.

Bombing raids in April and May 1941 left 100 homes so badly damaged they had to destroyed. Another 10,000 needed repair. A total of 83 people died and more than 300 were injured.

When you see the photographs of the damage it is amazing how much of the old town was saved and how people just seemed to shrug their shoulders and carry on with life. Boarded up shop windows with "business as usual" posters and salvaged furniture stacked on pavements were bizarre signs of the times.

Barrow townsfolk bore their difficulties together and celebrated their triumphs together.

Two sporting highlights – both at the famous old Wembley Stadium – stand out as putting a huge smile on Barrow's face.

In 1955 thousands of Barrovians turned the Rugby League Challenge Cup Final into a London holiday to remember.

Few who were there could ever forget the scenes as a victorious team returned home and was driven through packed Barrow streets to a civic reception at the town hall.

In 1990 it was football's turn to celebrate as Barrow AFC brought home the FA Trophy after a thrilling Final against Leek Town.

Both sporting triumphs were captured on some memorable *Evening Mail* photographs.

We hope they will bring back happy memories.

Shipbuilding continues to play a major part in the life of the town. Most Barrovians must have worked on, or know someone who played a part in the construction of, at least one of the ships or submarines we have featured.

Those chosen are merely a cross-section of the huge number of Barrow vessels launched in the past few decades.

The impact of major events at the yard has been felt throughout Furness.

When VSEL took over management of the yard in 1986 thousands of Barrow workers took part in the share offer.

And in 1988 when yard workers held mass meetings, marched through the town and stayed out on strike for weeks it brought normal life in Barrow to a standstill.

Alongside the major news events, the *Evening Mail's* photographers have captured for posterity all manner of more unusual events.

You can see circus elephants lumbering into town, the crowning of a king of Piel, a smoking contest, the arrival of the skateboard craze and the toppling of Barrow's brickworks chimney.

The weather never ceases to fascinate us and is featured in vintage pictures of snow and floods halting the traffic, lightning over the Barrow rooftops and ice blocks floating in Walney channel.

The *Evening Mail* made its own piece of Barrow history by celebrating a century of publication in 1998. The highlight of a year of centenary events was a visit to the *Mail's* Abbey Road head office by Queen Elizabeth.

Bill Myers
Assistant Editor (Production)
Evening Mail

Acknowledgements

Many *Evening Mail* colleagues have helped in the compilation of this book.

Special thanks goes to assistant librarian Sheila Atkinson for help in scanning the photographs and to Mike Rushton and Cheryl Draper for identifying locations on uncaptioned negatives.

Technical assistance in preparing the images for publication was provided by Jo Gardner, Val Boardley, Richard Britten, Ian Kershaw and Ben Crisp.

A final thanks goes to the many *Evening Mail* photographers who have been recording Barrow's people, places and events on film for the past 60 years. Without them this book would not have been possible.

To order photographs

Copies of any of the photographs within *Memory Lane Barrow* can be ordered through the *Evening Mail* offices at Newspaper House, Abbey Road, Barrow-in-Furness, Cumbria LA14 5QS.

Fun and Entertainment

Crowds stop to watch the Chipperfield's Circus elephants arrive at Barrow Railway Station in 1957.

John Whitehead from Snapdragon Circus balances on a 30ft-high tightrope in the Furness Abbey Amphitheatre in 1991.

Strongmen entertain the crowds in Ramsden Square during the 1950s.

The baby elephants proved a huge attraction when the circus came to town in the early 1960s.

In 1993 the fairground came to the heart of Barrow with a temporary site on the town hall car park.

When the sun shines Biggar Bank at Walney is a magnet to sun seekers. This picture dates from 1964.

The Black Knights parachute display team dropped in at Barrow's Rotary Gala in 1990.

Children having fun on the Barrow Park roundabout in 1973.

The swans and ducks have always appealed to youngsters visiting Barrow Park. This picture was taken in August 1963.

The final stages in preparing begonias for Barrow Park displays during the 1960s.

The Barrow Park ducks get a welcome winter feed in January 1992 as the lake freezes over.

Making a big splash at the old Biggar Bank public swimming pool in the 1960s.

The Biggar Bank pool was one of Walney's most popular attractions in the 1950s and 1960s, despite the water being cold.

This view from the late 1950s shows the Biggar Bank pool drained for renovation work.

Her Majesty's Theatre on the corner of Albert Street and Shore Street was one of Barrow's best-loved places of entertainment. It is shown here in the 1970s.

Stage builders at work on a production at Her Majesty's Theatre, Barrow, in 1964.

Like so many grand old buildings in Barrow, the bulldozers claimed Her Majesty's Theatre and reduced it to a pile of rubble in 1973.

Eliza, played by Margot Lewis, and Doolittle, played by Gordon Woodhouse, in the 1988 production of *My Fair Lady* by Walney Amateurs.

A scene from the Walney Amateurs' production of *Fiddler on the Roof* in 1995.

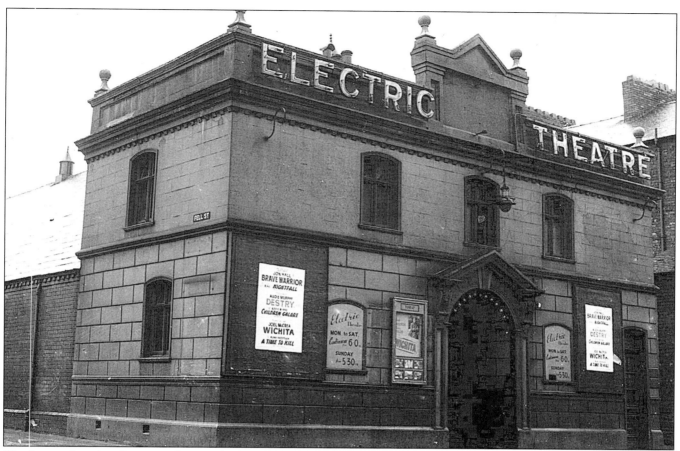

The impressive 1957 frontage of Barrow's Electric Cinema on the corner of Fell Street and Buccleuch Street. The site is now part of a car park.

The Regal Bar on Forshaw Street didn't look much from the outside but the old theatre and cinema was one of the town's oldest places of entertainment. This picture is from 1970.

You can catch a glimpse of the old splendour of the Regal Theatre in Forshaw Street as the demolition crews get to work in 1992.

If you asked Barrovians to vote for their favourite building the Coliseum would probably be neck and neck with the town hall. Unlike the town hall, this old cinema is now part of a car park.

The old Essoldo Cinema on Abbey Road in 1970. It was demolished and the site is now home to Jubilee House.

The Walney Cinema was finally demolished in 1985.

Up to the 1950s Walney had its own cinema where filmgoers thrilled to the exploits of Clark Gable and Vivien Leigh.

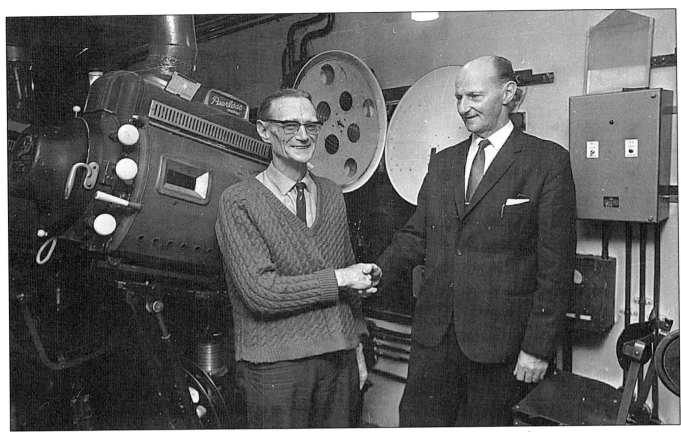

The projection room in the former Ritz Cinema on Abbey Road in 1973. The building now stands empty.

Staff pose outside the former Ritz Cinema in 1973.

Batman brought out the crowds to what was then called the Astra Cinema in 1989. More than 400 people queued along Holker Street to watch the first night.

The *Mutant Ninja Turtle*s was one of the big hit films of 1990 at the Astra Cinema on Abbey Road.

Action from a *Furness Mystery Play* staged in the Furness Abbey ruins in 1966.

The shipyard band in formal attire for a 1957 open-air concert.

Overalls were the standard uniform for practice sessions in the 1950s for the Vickers shipyard band.

Town Centre Redevelopment

Town centres change dramatically through time. This aerial view from the end of the 1960s shows Alfred Barrow School along with the distinctive crescent shape of the new Furness House.

Barrow has seen a series of major developments. Some were planned to clear decayed property or make way for grand plans while others were forced by dramatic events such as the Blitz of World War Two. Pictured here in 1968 are Duke Street shops facing the town hall on land needed for the Civic Hall and the Mall.

Paxton Terrace was another part of old Barrow living on borrowed time in 1968.

Cavendish Square shown in 1968. The shops were demolished and the statue of Lord Cavendish moved as builders created a new town centre for Barrow.

The old and the new share
the skyline in 1968. Furness
House in the background
towers over the threatened
Paxton Terrace.

The old Alexandra pub on
the Corner of Thomas Street
in 1962.

The alley off Paxton Street in 1968 with an old gas lamp and the side of the Snipe pub on the left.

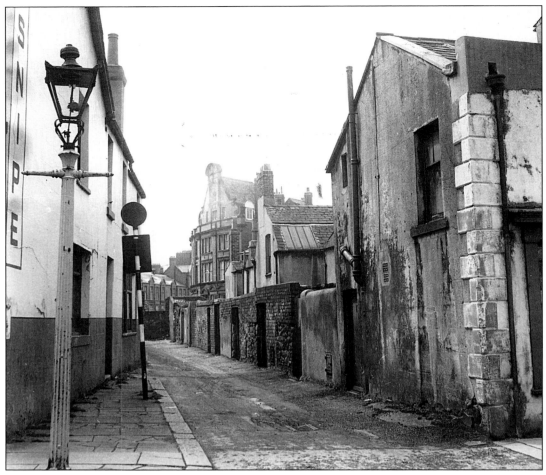

The Snipe pub features in this 1968 view of Paxton Street before the bulldozers arrived.

Barrow Town Hall towers over Paxton Street showing once familiar shops of the 1960s including the Scotch Bakery and Hunters.

When the demolition crews finally arrived the change to central Barrow was dramatic. Here Dot's Pantry and Parkinson's sweet shop are shown in ruins.

There are few things more attractive to small boys than a pile of rubble. Here are the remains of demolished town centre shops in 1968.

Another Paxton Street shop meets its fate under the watchful gaze of the town hall.

The debris left behind as properties were abandoned around Paxton Street as demolition work became inevitable.

Victor and vanquished in 1968. The new Furness House stands proud among the ruins of old shops.

This varied collection of 1960s cars found a temporary use for the town centre demolition site before new building work could get under way.

This unusual view from January 1969 shows youngsters walking through what would become the Mall and the new indoor market while behind them you can see the old town market.

The Cavendish Square statue is hoisted on to a lorry to make way for building work at the Civic Hall and the Mall in 1970.

Builders fitting out the stalls at Barrow's new indoor market in 1971.

The Queen opens Barrow's new indoor market in 1971.

Market Street in 1971 showing the side of the town hall and the old Barrow Market buildings.

Cornwallis Street, the town hall clock tower and the old Barrow outdoor market dominate the centre of this 1966 aerial view.

Barrow's old fish market in the 1940s. It was another building swept away in the town centre redevelopment of the late 1960s.

A classic 1961 view inside Barrow's old market on land now part of Cornwallis Street car park.

Shoppers hunting for the best deals on Barrow's old outdoor market in 1968.

Bargain hunters crowd the old Barrow indoor market in 1964.

The last day of trading at the old Barrow indoor market in 1971.

Go forward 20 years and the demolitions teams were back again. This time clearing the path for the Portland Walk shopping development. This 1992 picture shows part of Forshaw Street.

This view taken from the town hall clock tower in 1995 shows the Forshaw Street clearance area which is now beneath Portland Walk.

Building work under way on the Portland Walk shopping centre in 1996. The main framework of steel on the right would eventually become Debenhams.

Transport

A busy scene on Platform 2 at Barrow Railway Station in the 1950s.

In 1978 one of the world's best-loved steam locomotives *Flying Scotsman* came to Barrow shipyard as part of a major restoration project.

A view outside Barrow Railway Station shortly after the debris of the 1941 air raid was cleared away.

The interior of Barrow Railway Station after Blitz damage had taken away many of its finest architectural features, including the glass display case which held famed Furness Railway locomotive *Coppernob*.

Railways held the key to the development of Barrow as first an iron ore handling port and later a major European iron and steel manufacturer. This 1966 view shows the rail sidings at Barrow Docks.

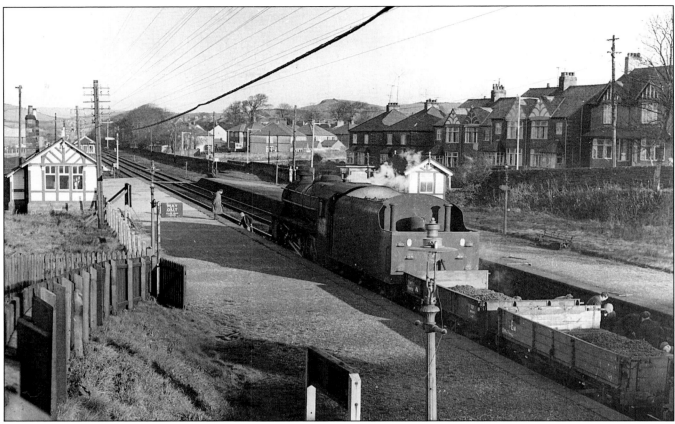

A railway line gang adding ballast under the railway lines passing through Roose Station in 1959.

Coppernob is one of Britain's oldest steam locomotives and until the end of the Victorian era it worked on the Furness Railway network. The locomotive was on display at Barrow until it was damaged in the Blitz. It is shown here on a return visit to Barrow in the 1960s.

In 1996 *Coppernob* made another return to Barrow Railway Station as part of celebrations for the 150th anniversary of the Furness Railway. It is now on permanent display at the National Railway Museum in York.

A Fordson tractor with driver and three farm workers shown around 1940. Today the work would be tackled by one man in a combine harvester.

The Stone Trough is still there but Abbey Road has changed greatly to cope with the needs of modern traffic since 1973.

Carr Lane on Walney sinks under flood water in 1962.

Barrow has always suffered its share of flooding problems. Here parked cars vanish beneath the rising water in 1989 on Low Road at the side of what is now the Tesco store.

Traffic coping with floods in Roose Road during the 1950s.

A motorist with an unusual load gets a push through the snow on Devonshire Road in 1995.

As an engineering town Barrow is used to seeing big loads slowly manoeuvring through the streets. This huge piece of equipment was heading to Rampside Gas Terminal in 1993.

Another large load shown in 1964. It was part of a mill built for Eastwoods Cement by Vickers-Armstrong Engineering in Barrow.

A wagon and trailers of the Barrow-based T. Brady & Sons haulage company shown in the 1970s.

Two women police officers shown with a patrol car in front of the old Barrow fish market and town hall.

Before local government changes in 1974 Barrow had its own education committee and school meals service. This van, with Milner's printworks behind, dates to around 1940.

Customers reading travel offers, including excursions to Piel Island, in this 1950s picture of the old Barrow Corporation travel office which faced the town hall and police station.

Traffic congestion is not a new feature in Barrow town centre. A parking warden makes his point on Crellin Street car park around 1970.

Bicycles and cars circle the Schneider Square statue around 1950 with the Furness Dining Rooms and the Leyland Paint and Varnish Company in the background.

A gleaming new 1940s double decker bus outside the town hall bearing the distinctive Barrow registration plate EO8652.

A busy traffic scene at the end of the Michaelson Road Bridge in the 1950s.

When a Barrow Corporation Transport bus broke down this 1950s recovery vehicle was sent to the rescue from its base on Hindpool Road.

The former Barrow Borough Transport bus depot on Hindpool Road in 1993. It was demolished to make way for car parking and a shopping development.

Life saving equipment being tested in the 1940s. A rocket system is shown which was designed to launch a rope to a ship in distress.

A BSA motorcycle and an old-style petrol pump at the Girling Garage in Barrow in the 1950s.

Barrow lifeboat *The Herbert Leigh* flying the flag in the 1940s.

A view of Walney's manned lighthouse in 1962.

One of Walney Lighthouse's best-known keepers was Peggy Braithwaite. She is shown being interviewed for a radio broadcast.

Huge blocks of ice float in Walney Channel during the severe winter conditions of January 1963.

Walney Lighthouse has to take the worst the weather can throw at it. Here it gets a new protective coat of paint in 1995. Principal lighthouse keeper Ian Clark (top) is shown with painters Shaun Charnley and Stephen Rawlinson.

Barrow in the 1940s still had a busy dockyard with cargoes bound for all parts of the world leaving regularly.

A hive of activity at Barrow docks as a timber cargo is unloaded in the 1950s.

Small boats moored in Walney Channel are still a familiar sight but the tall chimneys of Barrow's once great iron and steel industry have all vanished since this picture was taken around 1940.

In the early 1990s Barrow had its own airline called Air Furness.

The Barrow Blitz

During a few nights in April and May 1941 the full horror of modern warfare came to Barrow. The German bombing raids were designed to damage ships in the docks and disrupt production at the shipyard or steelworks. They mostly failed in those objectives but did cause civilian casualties and widespread damage to homes, shops and public buildings. More than 100 homes were so badly damaged they had to be demolished with more than 10,000 needing repair. A total of 83 people died in the Barrow Blitz and more than 300 were injured. To some degree the town authorities saw it coming and from 1938 air raid precaution drills were held in Barrow as this photograph shows.

Civilians also prepared for the coming world conflict. Here a few bottles of beer made the digging more enjoyable as a Barrow garden gets an Anderson shelter to protect against air raids.

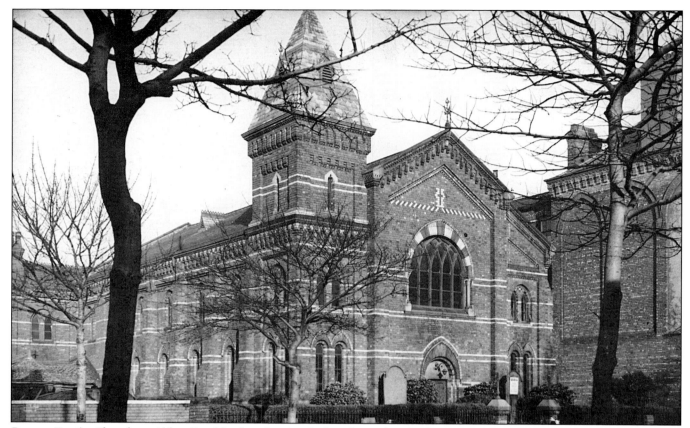

Barrow Baptist Church on Abbey Road in the calm days before the outbreak of war in September 1939. It was founded in 1873 and reduced to rubble in 1941.

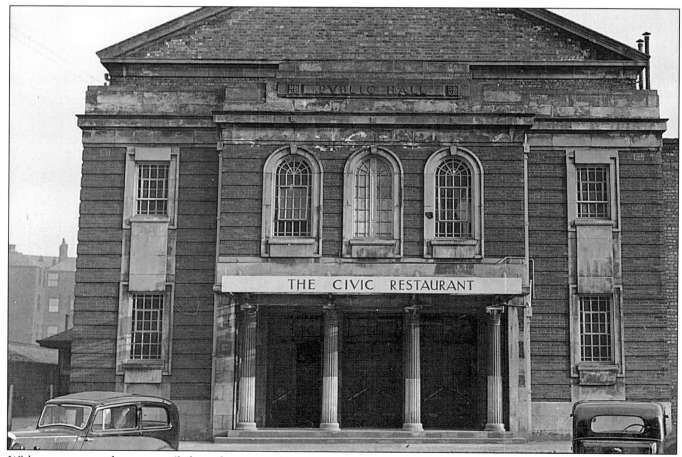

With so many people temporarily homeless, or unable to use damaged gas or electricity supplies to cook, the authorities set up a series of civic restaurants to provide meals. This one was based in the Public Hall, off Cornwallis Street.

The Duke of Kent came to visit Hindpool in July 1941. He is shown with mayor Alderman Brunskill talking with families whose homes had been damaged in air raids. The duke died in August 1942 in a flying accident.

The following 28 photographs show actual damage to Barrow homes and buildings during the Blitz raids of 14 to 16 April and 3 to 10 May. They are shown in the order they were taken by *North Western Daily Mail* photographers. Here shoppers walk past the bomb damaged public baths on Abbey Road. It is now the site of the Barrow Magistrates Court.

ARP units search the wreckage of the Trevelyan Hotel on Abbey Road. Several commercial travellers staying at the hotel were killed on 14 April.

Barrow's magnificent Victorian railway station is reduced to a broken shell. On the right is the ornate glass display case for original Furness Railway locomotive *Coppernob*.

The ruins of the Abbey Road Baptist Church. The building stood on what is now Coronation Gardens. The minister, Gilbert Mason, and a helper, Eric Davies, were killed while fire watching from the roof on 16 April.

Wardrobes and bedding on the pavement in Prospect Road as ARP teams salvaged all they could from the ruins.

Rescue workers clearing the debris in Vernon Street. You can see the roof of one of the town's many back street air raid shelters.

The Abbey baths suffered severe damage in the raids on 14 and 16 April. Here only the pool steps handrail on the right remains to show that this was a swimming pool.

Broken glass covers the pavement outside the cinema shops on Abbey Road. The sign with a large S points the way to a public air raid shelter.

Business as usual signs outside what is now the Travellers Rest Club on Abbey Road.

You can see the remnants of a ground floor metal bomb shelter on this picture of damaged homes in Hawcoat Lane.

A view through the ruined Abbey Road public baths in April 1941 towards the Shakespeare Street area.

A huge Leyland wagon is used to take away fallen beams as rescue crews clear the site of the Trevelyan Hotel.

A hand basin, table and chair cling to what remains of a bedroom floor in the Trevelyan Hotel on Abbey Road.

Rescue teams at work in Union Street.

Back Vernon Street and Back Collingwood Street on 14 April. Eighteen people were killed in the street during this raid and on 7 May. A total of 18 houses were destroyed or had to be demolished.

The entire roof and upper floor has collapsed on this Vernon Street home. Part of Vernon Street was completely rebuilt after the war.

Rescue teams at work in Vernon Street. During hectic activity on 14 April a pair of ambulances were sent to Vernon Street at 3.32am. The siren for the all clear went 10 minutes later.

Bomb blast protection on shop windows in Dalton Road during the Blitz.

Bedroom windows hang in place precariously on this pair of houses in Holker Street.

Bedrooms are left open to the road like a giant dolls'-house in this picture of bomb damage in Baldwin Street.

Not a window unbroken or a slate in place on this section of Suffolk Street.

Furniture piled up outside the ruins of a home in Suffolk Street.

The *Evening Mail*, then the *North Western Daily Mail*, suffered along with the other buildings on Abbey Road caught up in the raid of 16 April. The offices suffered blast damage but still managed to produce a newspaper that night.

Severe damage to homes on Suffolk Street caused on 3 May. The ambulance teams set up their base to treat casualties in a nearby gospel hall.

Exmouth Street and Blake Street were hit on 3 May in a raid aimed at industrial targets. More than 50 houses in the area were destroyed or had to pulled down as unsafe.

Attempts to salvage furniture from homes in Hawcoat Lane, off Undergreens Road. This area was hit on 7 May.

A scene of devastation in Undergreens Road on 7 May.

Staff pose in the doorway of the *North Western Daily Mail* offices on Abbey Road. This picture, like others from the *Mail's* archive of Blitz material, was taken under strict conditions. None were published during the war to prevent the enemy knowing what damage had been caused. Barrow raids were simply described as 'damage to a north west town.' Only those who lived through it really knew what it was like.

Barrow Rugby League

Thousands of sport-mad Barrovians turned the 1955 Rugby League Challenge Cup Final into a triumphant London holiday. Winning the cup for the first time only added to the holiday feeling. Here Barrow fans are shown in London's Trafalgar Square.

Private car ownership was still a novelty in 1955 so the bulk of Barrow's support made the trip to Wembley by coach or train. This picture was taken on the rugby special train to Euston.

You couldn't celebrate anything in style in Barrow without a bottle of James Thompson's finest ale. There was plenty to go round when Barrow won the cup.

Two young fans on the London train with their traditional wooden rattles and rosettes.

Were you among the thousands who travelled to Wembley to cheer on Barrow in the 1955 Final? Barrow won in front of 66,513 spectators.

Captain Willie Horne was Barrow's star player and inspiration in the 1955 Cup Final. The town mourned his death in March 2001, at the age of 79 years.

The Barrow players arrived back at Barrow Railway Station as heroes.

Barrow players hold aloft Willie Horne and the Challenge Cup after beating Workington in the Final by 21 points to 12.

The Challenge Cup was shown to Barrow fans from an open-top coach.

Here the team coach passes the old Palace Cinema, now Wilkinsons, on Duke Street.

Barrow fans of all ages celebrated the 1955 Challenge Cup victory well into the night.

Willie Horne gets a celebration kiss from his mother outside the town hall.

Jimmy Lewthwaite (right) was one of Barrow Rugby League Club's greats. He was an unstoppable right-wing in the 1940s and 1950s and was an Australian tourist for Great Britain.

A typical action pose from the greatest of all Barrow Rugby League players Willie Horne. His opponents at club or international level never knew what he would do next.

Barrow failed to repeat the success of 1955 two years later and narrowly lost in the Challenge Cup final to Leeds by nine points to seven. The team still received a civic welcome.

The club returned to the twin towers of Wembley in 1967 but lost by 17 points to 12 against Featherstone Rovers. Here a group of Barrow fans dress the part for the London trip.

Skirts above the knee and Cilla Black hair-styles were all the rage for Barrow fans at the 1967 Challenge Cup Final.

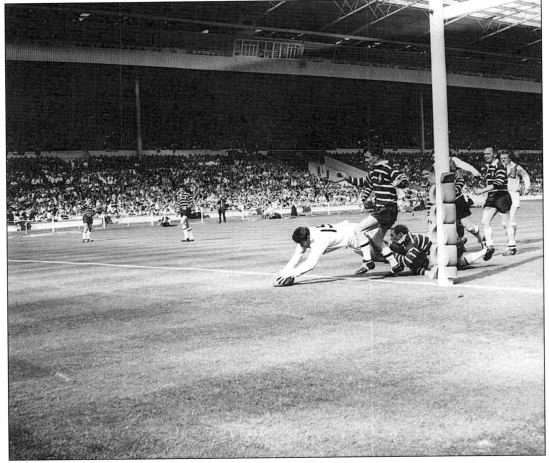

Action from the 1967 Final as Barrow loose-forward Mike Watson dives over the line to score.

Barrow players being introduced to the Duke of Edinburgh before the kick-off for the 1967 Challenge Cup Final.

A team picture of the Barrow Rugby League team in October 1970.

Fans cheer on Barrow when the team took on Castleford in the second round of the Rugby League Challenge Cup in February 1970. Barrow lost by four points to 12 to the cup holders.

Despite the rain and the losing scoreline these Barrow fans were not down-hearted at the cup match against Castleford in 1970.

A Barrow player is tackled just short of the try-line in the Challenge Cup match against Castleford in 1970.

The victorious Barrow RL line up at the start of the Lancashire Cup Final of 1983 against Widnes. Shown (from left) are Tommy Dawes (coach), Alan Hodkinson (captain), Steve Tickle, Terry Moore, Andy Whittle, Ian Ball, Dave Milby, Ralph McConnell, David Cairns, Les Wall, Mark McJennett, Steve Herbert, Eddie Szymala, Steve Mossop, David Elliott and Kevin James.

These three Barrow fans are in fine voice at the Lancashire Cup Final against Widnes in 1983.

Eddie Szymala was Barrow's best-known impact player of the modern era. A player to make the fans gasp either in the tackle or running with the ball. He was a Great Britain international and part of Barrow's winning 1983 Lancashire Cup team.

Gary Broadbent is Barrow's latest export to the big time. Currently the Salford full-back in the Super League, he has also played for Widnes and went on tour to New Zealand with the Great Britain Academy Squad.

The future of all professional clubs is with youth. Here is the Victoria Junior School team, winners of the Dean Marwood rugby league trophy in 1997. The back row (from left): Steven Soulsby, Daniel McDonald, Alex Hughes, Andrew Adams, Jon Mason, Aaron Hughes and Danny Austin. Front row: Daniel Clawson, Robbie Morris, Mark Callow, Stewart McCullough (captain), Philip Coombe, Graham Capstick and Nathan Johnson.

This Sporting Town

Barrow Association Football Club celebrates a century in 2001 and without question its finest hour came at Wembley Stadium in 1990 as winners of the FA Trophy. Here Barrow fans are shown in front of the famous Wembley twin towers.

This young fan holds his treasured programme from the historic day on Saturday 19 May, when Barrow defeated Leek Town by 3-0 to lift the FA Trophy.

Barrow centre-half Kenny Gordon heading home one of his two goals in the FA Trophy triumph.

Barrow AFC manager Ray Wilkie and player Glenn Skivington discuss a job well done after the FA Trophy win. Ray Wilkie was to die aged just 56 and is commemorated by Wilkie Road outside Barrow's Holker Street ground.

Colin Cowperthwaite holds the FA Trophy aloft at Wembley. He scored one of the team's three goals to secure a memorable win for Barrow.

Barrow AFC on an open-top bus tour of Barrow with the FA Trophy. Thousands lined the streets to greet the cup winners.

Holker Street packed with cheering Barrow fans during the town's 1967 centenary celebrations.

The Barrow AFC team shown at Holker Street in the 1968 season.

Barrow defeated Burscough by a goal to nil at Morecambe in October 1982 to win the Cambrian Cup. An 82nd minute penalty kick by Colin Cowperthwaite decided the destination of the trophy.

Happy fans at Holker Street as Barrow beat Altrincham in a 1988 FA Trophy replay.

Barrow's most successful sportsman in terms of medals and sporting honours is footballer Emlyn Hughes. He signed for Liverpool from Blackpool in 1967 for a then record fee for a defender of £65,000. He became Liverpool and England Captain in the era when the Merseyside club dominated the English and European game.

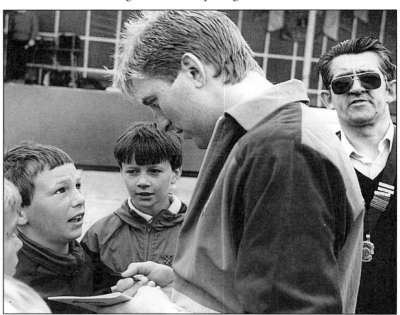

Another Barrow player to reach the top of the soccer tree was Gary Stevens, shown here signing autographs before opening a Furness Lions garden and music festival in 1987. He made his Everton debut in 1985 and became a regular in England's defence. He later signed for Glasgow Rangers.

The Barrow Celtic Under-16 football team celebrate winning four trophies in the 1994 season. On the back row are (from left) Leigh Doyle, Robert Bradley, Robert Rennie, Stewart Backen, Dave Canavan and Darren Wakefield. On the front row are Michael Smith, Glenn Knagg, Michael Martin, Stuart Welsh and Martyn Conroy.

Long queues form outside the Holker Street football ground in 1973 to watch motorcycle action with Barrow's speedway riders.

Speedway riders on the start line at Holker Street in 1973.

Yachting has always had a popular following in Barrow. This 1960 view shows a yacht in Walney Channel with the steelworks chimneys behind.

Action at the Barrow bowling rink in the 1950s.

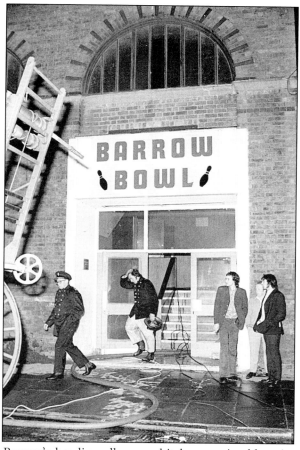

Barrow's bowling alley was hit by a major blaze in 1972.

The diving boards at the Abbey Road public pool during the 1960s. The pool was eventually demolished and replaced with a new pool at Barrow Leisure Centre in the public park.

The Barrow Beavers swimming club's most illustrious member was Simone Hindmarch. She swam the first leg in the English medley relay squad which won gold in the Edinburgh Commonwealth Games of 1986.

Barrow swimmer Shaun Uren who won a silver medal in the 1996 Paralympic Games in Atlanta, USA.

Barrow mountain bike rider Caroline Alexander who represented Great Britain in the Atlanta Games.

Back in 1948 these three Barrow Olympic athletes were pictured at the Strawberry Grounds. Pictured are (from left) 110m hurdler Joe Birrell, 5,000m runner Alan Parker and long jumper Harry Askew. Joe Birrell and Harry Askew represented Great Britain in the 1948 London Olympics while Alan Parker competed at Helsinki in 1952.

Barrow hurdler Joe Birrell is seen in action before representing Great Britain at the 1948 London Olympics.

Chetwynde School captain Sarah Harrison in contention with the Australian keeper Tanya Meldrum (front) during a 1992 game between the school and a touring Australian school side.

The Victoria Junior School cricket team pictured in the 1980s.

The oval of Vickerstown Cricket Ground is prominent on this aerial picture of Walney from 1970. Behind the central group of houses is now the Park Vale athletics stadium, next to the Periscope pub.

Champion body builder and Furness Health Studios founder Bill Hemsworth is shown on the right of this 1974 photograph. Among his titles was Mr Universe.

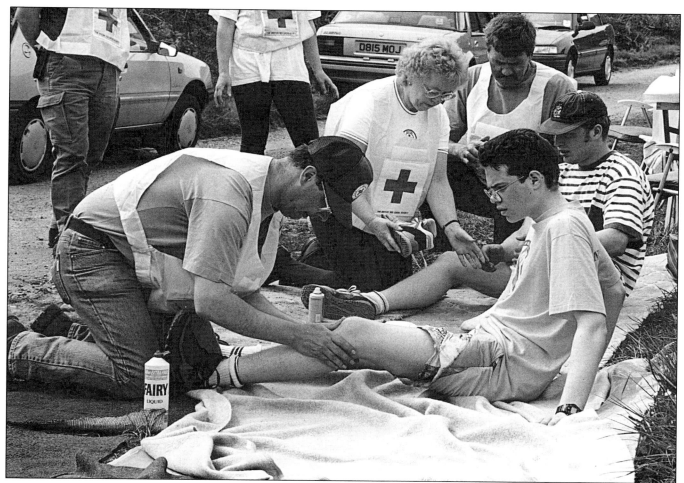

Sport for all could be the motto of the Keswick to Barrow Walk where hundreds test their endurance on a 40-mile route which raises thousands of pounds for Furness charities. This view of the medical staff in action helping the walking wounded is from 1993.

The venue is Barrow Public Hall and the event is the final of the *Evening Mail* darts championships in April 1970. The winner was Ray Hendley while the eventual loser was the public hall – demolished during a 1990s phase of town centre redevelopment.

In the Headlines

Princess Elizabeth of York, later the Queen Mother, in Barrow during 1935 for the renaming ceremony for Walney's Jubilee Bridge.

Huge crowds in Cavendish Square to greet the Queen and the Duke of Edinburgh in 1956.

The Queen waves to the crowds from the Barrow Town Hall balcony during a visit to the town, accompanied by the Duke of Edinburgh in 1956.

A policeman stands guard as the Queen leaves the town hall in 1956.

The Queen leaving the Barrow-built ocean liner *Oriana*, after a tour of the luxury ship during a 1960 visit to Barrow.

A jumbo-sized dishwasher is shown to the Queen in 1960 in the galley of the liner *Oriana*.

Princess Margaret visits Barrow during the borough centenary celebrations in 1967.

Three patriotic youngsters get ready to wave their flags for Princess Margaret during her 1967 visit to Barrow.

Crowds climb the base of the Cavendish statue in Cavendish Square to get a good view of Princess Margaret in June 1967.

A huge fireworks display was held in Barrow as part of the borough centenary celebrations in 1967.

Youngsters wait expectantly for the start to the 1967 borough centenary fireworks show.

Barrovians bring a smile to the face of Queen Elizabeth during a visit to open Furness General Hospital on 24 May in 1985.

The Queen on one of her first walkabouts during a visit to Barrow in 1971 to launch HMS *Sheffield* and open the town's new market hall.

Diana, Princess of Wales, at the Commissioning ceremony for HMS *Vanguard* in August 1993.

Demonstrators call for the end of H-bomb tests on a 1962 march through Barrow. Barrow's nuclear submarine building programme attracted many peace and political groups to the town.

Ban the bomb marchers in Barrow during 1962.

Campaign for Nuclear Disarmament marchers protest against the Barrow Polaris submarine programme in 1966.

Demonstrators
make their point
at a Save our
Shore march in
1968.

Strikers picket the
North Western
Gas Board depot
on Hindpool
Road in 1973.
This year was one
of widespread
industrial
disruption.

Health unions on the picket line outside the old Roose Hospital in 1973.

Few demonstrations challenged this for size. The Campaign for Nuclear Disarmament mass 'die in' to challenge the Trident submarine programme in 1984.

CND protesters take part in a lie-down protest during the naming ceremony for *Vanguard* at VSEL in 1992.

Police officers clearing anti-nuclear protesters to reopen the road outside the Devonshire Dock Hall in 1992.

The successful campaign to save the Fell Street public toilets took to the streets in 1997.

Fire crews in action at the Cavendish Furniture Company showrooms on Duke Street in 1956. The shop is now Dandy's Beds.

A blaze at the old North Lonsdale Hospital in 1988.

A fire and explosion at the Gas and Coke Works on Abbey Road, Barrow, in the 1950s.

Crowds of workmen look on as firemen begin the clear-up after an explosion and fire at the Abbey Road Gas and Coke Works.

A spectacular lightning show over the Rawlinson Street brewery tower in 1963.

Electronic speed traps come to Duke Street, Barrow, in April 1979.

A dramatic show of flags and smoke during the Barrow Town Hall Tattoo to mark the building's centenary in 1987.

Pupils leaving the old Walney School for the final time in February 1993.

Barrow's Terry Goulding waits for an evaluation on his three elephant statues at the *Antiques Roadshow* in 1993.

When the popular BBC Television show *Antiques Roadshow* came to Barrow Leisure Centre in 1993 it brought out thousands of people to find out more about their attic treasures.

Children at Vickerstown School took a step back in time when they were visited by the Hautbois Musicians in October 1997 to recreate the music and dress of the Tudor and Victorian eras.

Bringing You the News

A visit by the Queen provided the highlight for the *Evening Mail's* centenary celebrations in 1998. Here she is greeted outside Newspaper House by (from left) Tony Raymond, managing director of Furness Newspapers, CN Group chief executive Robin Burgess and chairman Joe Harris.

The Queen receives flowers from well-wishers as she arrives at Newspaper House for an official visit to mark the *Evening Mail's* centenary year.

Crowds line Abbey Road to watch the Queen visit the *Evening Mail* head office on 20 February 1998.

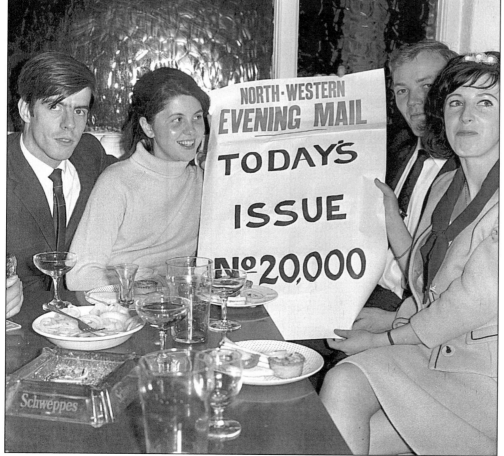

Celebrations for the 20,000th issue of the *Evening Mail* in 1965. The first issue was published on 1 January 1898.

The paper takes its community role seriously and helps a number of good causes each year through the CN Group Charitable Trust. Here newspaper sales and marketing director Lyndsay Aspin hands over £200 to youngsters from the Dale Street Nursery in Ulverston.

The *Evening Mail* Fun Day in Barrow Park was born as a fund-raising device for the £180,000 appeal to open a NSPCC child protection centre in Barrow. This view of action from the raft race was taken in July 1993.

Fund-raising for the *Evening Mail*/NSPCC appeal took many forms. Here Nick Conway (Billy from the popular television comedy *Bread*) signs autographs for fans at a celebrity football match at Holker Street in 1993. By 2001 the appeal had raised more than £225,000.

By 1992 the *Evening Mail* was one of a dwindling number of newspapers yet to fully embrace the computer age. This view is of reporters and sub-editors at work.

When the change came it was dramatic. Here is the same office a few weeks later.

Linotype operators at work setting metal type to make up the individual lines of text for pages of the *Evening Mail* in 1976. This process has now been consigned to history by computer technology. Shown are (from left) Terry Horne, David Barker (obscured) Ted Atkinson and David McKegg.

An *Evening Mail* stereotyper producing a semi-circular metal printing plate in 1965.

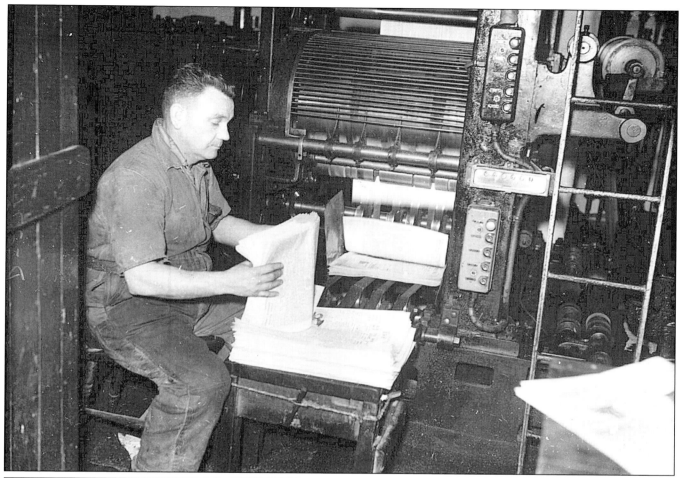

Copies of the *Evening Mail* come off the press in Abbey Road in the 1950s. The papers were bundled and dispatched from the back door in High Street.

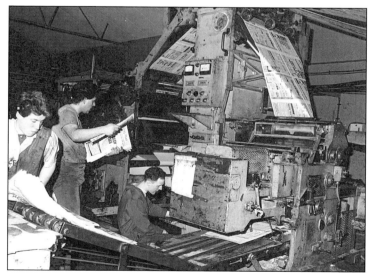

A busy scene as the presses roll in the new *Evening Mail* press hall in Emlyn Street in March 1992.

Sparks fly as the old *Evening Mail* rotary press is cut up in 1988. It marked the end of printing newspapers in the company's Abbey Road head office.

New printing press equipment arrives at the *Evening Mail* in March 1995. Shown with it are press hall staff (from left) Curtis Pattinson, Brian Elliott, Kevin Hall, David Moffatt, James Haney, Steve Ireland, Graham McQuistan and Paul Hall.

This picture shows an *Evening Mail* delivery van driver at work in 1965.

The *Mail* aims to deliver whatever the South Cumbria weather. Here delivery driver Jim Hancox waits for help after heavy snow in February 1996.

This picture book has only been possible because tens of thousands of *Evening Mail* negatives, photographs – and now digital images – have been stored and cared for over the past 60 years. Shown are the paper's chief librarian Heather Horner (left) and assistant librarian Sheila Atkinson in 1997.

Reasons to Celebrate

Bunting links the shops in Dalton Road, Barrow, as part of the celebrations for the Queen's coronation in 1953.

Royal plaques cover the walls of McAdam's fashion store and the Cavendish furniture showroom on Duke Street for the 1953 coronation.

Ramsden Square roundabout is decorated for the coronation celebrations in 1953.

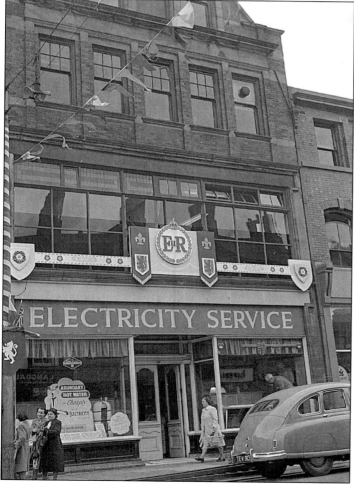

The Rediffusion electrical store decorated for the coronation in 1953.

The North Western Electricity Board showroom on the corner of Duke Street and Cavendish Street in 1953. The site was cleared to make way for a council housing office.

Cups of tea for all at this Barrow party for the 1953 coronation. Dozens of streets held outdoor events or made use of church and village halls for parties.

Paper hats helped to get youngsters in the mood for fun at this coronation party in 1953.

The weather proved kind to this outdoor coronation party in Barrow.

Arthur Street decorated with bunting and packed with people keen to enjoy themselves for the silver jubilee in 1977.

Barrow celebrated in style for the Queen's silver jubilee in 1977. Most of the streets in town had an event or issued children with a commemorative of some kind. Shown here are celebrations in Arthur Street.

It was street party time again in May 1995 as Barrow joined the rest of Britain in celebrating 50 years since the end of World War Two in Europe. Pictured here is Lowther Crescent on Walney.

Asda staff join the VE Day anniversary celebrations. Shown are (from left) Sharron, Joanne, Fiona, Maureen, Lorraine, Lisa, David and Marie.

Staff and regulars at the Vic Vaults pub in Barrow join the VE Day anniversary celebrations. The event raised £1,700 to buy a special wheelchair.

Residents of Athol Street and Abercorn Street on Barrow Island during the VE Day anniversary celebrations.

Flags and uniforms for Furness General Hospital catering staff who cooked a traditional British menu to help mark 50 years since VE Day.

The Barrow mayor's parade passes the Brewery Inn on Cavendish Street in the 1940s.

Barrow's carnival queen leads a parade into the Craven Park rugby league ground around 1950.

Humpty Dumpty hoped for a mouth filled with pennies during this Barrow Hospitals carnival parade from around 1950.

Youngsters during a Barrow parade in the 1950s.

A clown keeps his balance on a bicycle in a 1950s carnival parade on the junction of Dalton Road and Abbey Road.

Margaret was carnival queen on this picture of the royal float on Dalton Road in the 1950s.

Parade floats were elaborate creations in the 1950s. This steam locomotive passes the Derby pub on Dalton Road.

Walney parade passes along Black Butts Lane in 1997.

Barrow shipyard had its own beauty queen in 1967 with the title Miss Vickers.

A king of Piel is crowned in an ancient and curious ceremony involving an old sword, a rusty helmet and plenty of beer.

Youngsters in Newbarns could celebrate a day off school thanks to polling day in 1983.

The skateboard craze reaches Parkview School in 1988.

Traditions die hard for these two contestants in a 1983 pipe smoking championship.

Barrow old soldiers remember fallen comrades in the Remembrance Day parade to Barrow park's cenotaph in 1997.

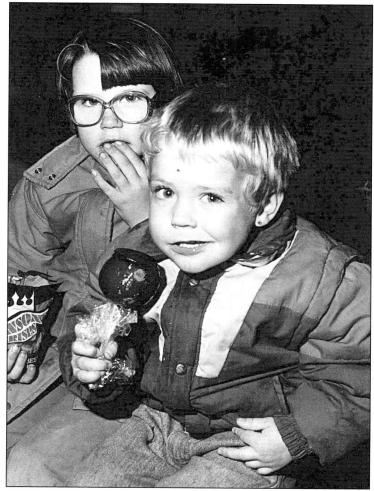

Andrew Atkins enjoys a toffee apple while Naomi Young prefers crisps as the perfect accompaniment to the Round Table fireworks display at Craven Park in 1989.

The Changing Face of Barrow

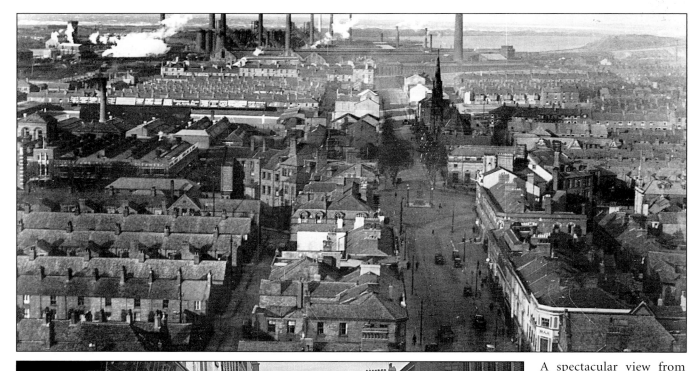

A spectacular view from Barrow Town Hall tower from around 1940 looking down Duke Street towards Ramsden Square and St Mary's Church with the steelworks chimneys in the background.

You can see Marks and Spencer on the right of this Dalton Road shopping scene from 1964.

The bottom section of Dalton Road during the 1950s with a gas lamp on the right and the old Story jeweller's shop clock on the left.

Mrs Woodruff (centre) watches as Marjorie Stockton (left) and Patricia Atkinson dress models at Woodruffs in Dalton Road during 1966. The business had been started in Ainslie Street just after World War Two.

The Woolworth store and Timpson's shoe shop on Dalton Road in the 1970s.

End of an era for Dalton Road as the last gas lamp is removed in 1970.

Shoppers queue for bargains at the original Dalton Road Tesco store on the corner of what is now the Portland Walk development.

Much has changed in the bottom half of this aerial view of Barrow in 1970. At the very bottom Caird's Foundry has given way to the new Tesco store. Just above it is the old corporation bus depot and the Lakeland Laundry – both largely gone to make way for shopping developments.

There wasn't much you couldn't buy at Pass and Company. Musical instruments, electrical goods and sporting equipment were specialities. The Duke Street building, shown here around 1950, is now home to the Yates's Wine Lodge.

A relatively traffic-free scene in Duke Street in the 1950s. Casualties of change of the left-hand row include Horne's wine merchants, the Inglenook Café and Lloyds Bank.

The bottom section of Crellin Street, just up from Rawlinson Street, in the late 1960s. Hannay's fishing tackle shop on the left will be familiar to many Barrovians.

This late 1960s view shows the top section of Crellin Street, facing the side of what is now the McDonald's restaurant.

Cavendish Street in the 1950s looking towards the Buccleuch Street power station cooling tower. You can see the former Odeon cinema on the left of the street.

You would have to be fast today to push a pram across the busy junction between the top of Dalton Road and Church Street. This picture is from 1956.

The opening of the Asda supermarket on Walney Road in the early 1970s was the biggest change to Barrow's shopping habits in a century. Here Cllr John Dick and wife Maureen open a new-look section of the store in 1988.

The Cross Keys has survived Barrow's redevelopments for the past thirty years but its neighbour the Ebenezer Methodist Chapel on William Street is now part of Debenhams. This picture is from around 1940.

Inside the old Travellers Rest pub on Dalton Road in January 1990. It was demolished to make way for Portland Walk shopping centre.

Frank Wood the men's outfitters and hat shop was a Barrow institution and another of the firms to vanish after 1990 to make way for Portland Walk. The shop opened in 1900 with a supply of Baden-Powell hats in honour of the famous victor at the Siege of Mafeking. Nigel Wood is shown in the doorway.

Assistant Lisa Gibson behind the counter at the Barrow Pet Stores on Forshaw Street in 1990.

A view along Forshaw Street in 1992 with the shops closed and boarded up ready for the bulldozers to arrive.

Workmen clearing snow from the old Michaelson Road Bridge in the 1950s.

Houses near completion on the Rainey Park estate in January 1964.

Building work under way on the new Barrow Sixth Form College in 1979.

An old cycle repair shop shown around 1940 on the corner of Wesley Place.

This early 1950s view shows the old Albion Hotel and the backs of Vickers offices on land near Fisher Street and the Strand.

The old Roose Hospital, the town's former workhouse. A fine building which couldn't find a new use after a health reorganisation left it empty and unwanted.

Children fascinated by the photographer in 1966 with the Barrow Island flats in the background.

A quiet country view of Roosecote Farm on Dungeon Lane in the 1950s.

The Victoria Park Hotel shown in 1970.

A view inside the ballroom at the Victoria Park Hotel in 1981.

All in a Day's Work

The chimney topples at Barrow brickworks in 1972. It stood on Walney Road, facing what is now the Asda site.

A Barrow coalman at work in the 1950s. Many town centre homes had coal chutes or backyard coal houses.

The Case's Brewery in Cavendish Street during the 1960s. The Buccleuch Street power station cooling tower is in the background.

The staff of BBC Radio Furness put the new station on the air from offices in Hartington Street in 1982.

A worker at the Listers textile factory in Roose from 1969.

Barrow Borough Council members at work in the town hall council chamber in the 1950s.

Construction workers bringing gas supplies to Rampside and Roa Island in 1992.

Pumping oxygen through the holding tanks at the Walney oyster nursery in 1989.

Tractor driver D. Williams of Walney at work on Roosecote Farm.

Cheese making in the 1950s at Roose Dairy.

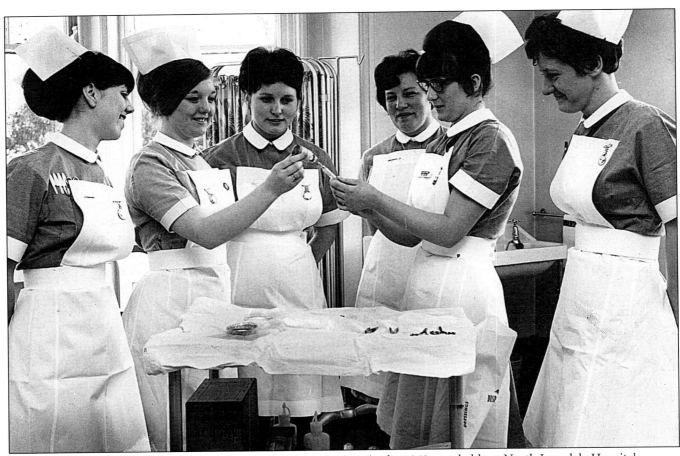

A group of trainee nurses learning correct technique for injections in the 1960s, probably at North Lonsdale Hospital.

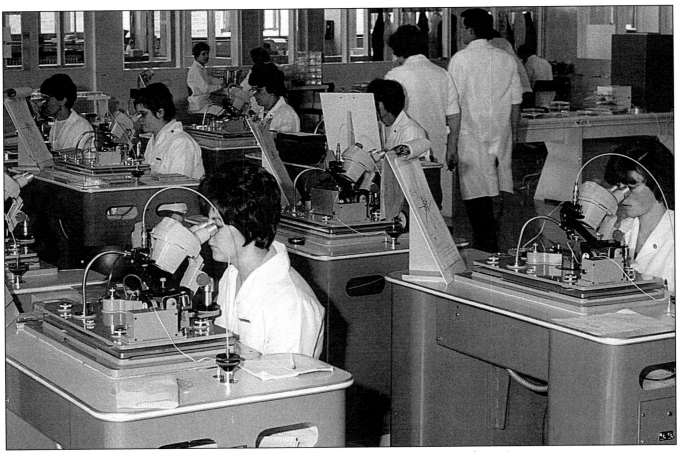

Microscopes were needed at the Ferranti factory in the 1960s to work on tiny integrated circuits.

The Ferranti factory in Ormsgill, Barrow, shown in December 1966.

The Crown Works of the Barrow Printing Company on the corner of Cornwallis Street during the 1960s.

Gordon Hewson working on a monotype casting machine at the Barrow Printing Company in the 1960s.

A view of the Barrow Paper Mills in 1948.

Heavy hand-powered machinery in use at a Barrow forming and assembly shop during the 1950s.

Workers on a flood prevention scheme on the Greengate Street side of Barrow Public Park in the 1960s.

The Bowater-Scott paper mill on Park Road in September 1968.

Workers stand in front of the new No 2 paper making machine at the Bowater-Scott mill in 1969. Shown (from left) are Colin Henry, Michael Hamilton, Bob Lambton, Bill Evans, Keith Finnegan, John Cormack, Russ Jenkins and Albert Joy.

The British Cellophane plant on Park Road. It closed in 1991 and was demolished to make way for a new candle factory.

Tim Clark (right) and Keith Logan shown on the last day of production at the British Cellophane plant in September 1991.

The British Cellophane chimney is toppled by demolition crews from Connell Brothers in July 1995.

Jeff Rigg, Brian Parkinson, John Fitzwilliam and Jimmy Howard watch over the molten iron in 1987 at the David Caird's Foundry. It was demolished to make way for Barrow's Tesco store.

The once familiar skyline across Barrow Ironworks. This picture was taken in November 1963 when it had been bought by C. Cooper Limited of West Bromwich.

You can almost feel the heat on this 1960s view inside Barrow Ironworks.

Sparks fly at Barrow Steelworks in the early 1980s. By then the plant was a shadow of its former self and waiting for closure.

Tapping the furnace inside Barrow Ironworks in the 1960s.

Casting ingots of molten metal at Barrow Steelworks in the 1960s.

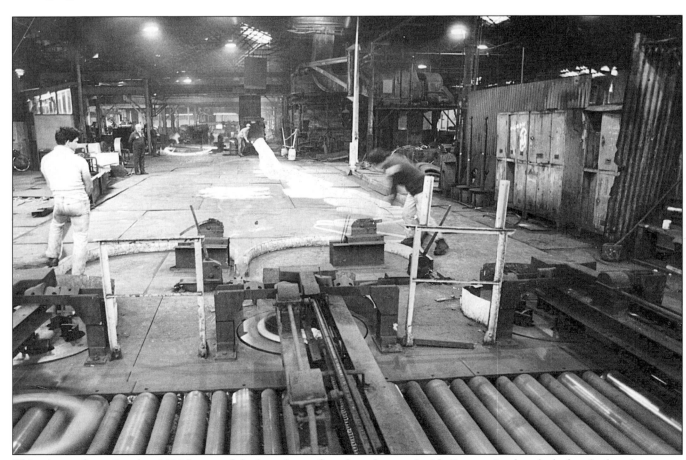

This picture from October 1983 is one of the last views of work under way inside Barrow Steelworks before it closed.

The huge sheet of metal hanging from chains offers some protection to workers from the fierce heat of molten metal at Barrow Steelworks in the 1960s.

The Barrow Steelworks offices in the 1960s showing one of the impressive chimneys which once dominated the Barrow skyline.

The Barrow Steelworks closing party in November 1983. It marked a symbolic end to the iron and steel industry which was the driving force behind the growth of Victorian Furness.

A Barrow Steelworks chimney topples in March 1985.

By June 1984 the Barrow Steelworks was an empty shell surrounded by dereliction. The site was later reborn as Project Furness, providing new factories, offices and showrooms.

Workers enjoying a high vantage point as they work to dismantle another Barrow iron industry chimney in January 1989.

Roosecote power station opened in the late 1950s. It cost £8 million and was built on what was a rifle range.

A detailed industrial scene on the railway sidings through the town gasworks around 1940.

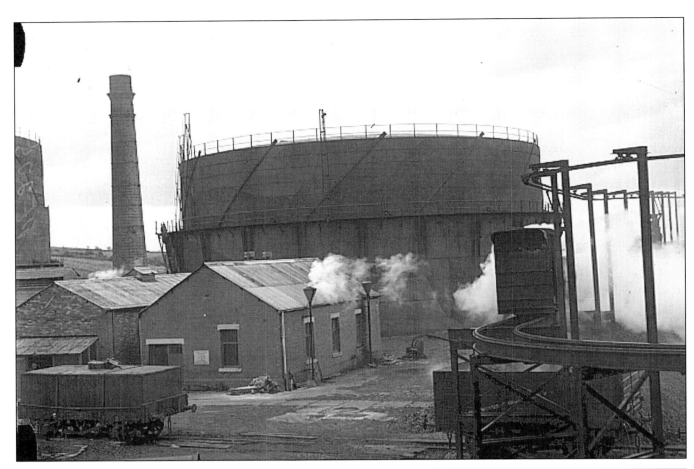

Tar was a by-product of the old Hindpool gasworks. One of the special rail containers to carry it is shown on the left.

The Barrow Corporation electricity works at Buccleuch Street in the 1940s.

Life in the Shipyard

A view across the workshop roofs at Vickers leading to the High Level Bridge in 1966.

Time to go home in 1957 as yard workers cross the High Level Bridge in their thousands.

A lone fisherman at peace with the world in 1957 with a part-finished ship under the Vickers cranes in the background.

Shipyard workers prepare the Vickers slipway for a launch just after World War Two.

A submarine and a ship under construction in 1970 with the shipyard workshops and Barrow Island flats in the background.

Shipyard workers in March 1957 with the tanker *British Glory* in the background. The 21,000-ton ship was built for the Tanker Charter Company and launched in February 1957.

A view inside the Vickers workshops in September 1969.

A 1960s picture showing the Vickers shipbuilding stocks from Walney Channel.

The engine machine shop at Vickers gives an indication of the scale of operations in 1950.

The 1,000th Sulzer engine shown at Vickers in October 1964.

VSEL draughtswoman Amanda Dyson became Miss Great Britain in 1988.

The television cameras came to film in Vickers in 1957. An overhead hoist, known in the yard as 'John's Rag Cart' was used to give the camera crew a bird's-eye view.

Sir Leonard Redshaw, managing director of Vickers Shipbuilding Group. He died in 1989.

A BBC cameraman at work in the shipyard during April 1957.

A shipyard crane in the 1960s. The mass of cranes was one of the dominant visual features of Barrow, along with the steelworks chimneys.

The engineering section at Vickers-Armstrongs made all manner of weird and wonderful metal fabrications. This 1960s big load was of cement machinery.

This piece of stone heritage was pictured by the shipyard main gate in 1994. It shows the arms of the original Barrow Ship Building Company founded in 1872.

A dramatic view of the Devonshire Dock Hall taking shape in the mid-1980s. It featured a massive £50 million shiplift capable of lifting 24,300-tonnes.

Going home time from the yard in March 1982.

This picture over the Barrow rooftops gives an idea of the huge scale of the Devonshire Dock Hall. It is 269 metres in length and just over 50 metres tall.

Workers at the Vickers shipyard gates in the 1950s.

Shipyard staff celebrate the successful VSEL Consortium bid to take over control of the company in 1986.

Putting the finishing touches to an AS90 self-propelled gun at Vickers in June 1986.

Workers leaving VSEL over the Michaelson Road Bridge in 1990.

Shipyard managing director Dr Rodney Leach led the VSEL Consortium which took over management of the shipyard in 1986.

Barrow shipyard has seen a number of bitter industrial disputes. Here strikers are shown in March 1957.

Workers head for home after a 1957 dispute ends in strike action.

Union leaders on the platform at a mass meeting of workers in August 1988. Shown (from left) are Frank Ward, Roger Henshaw and (far right) Keith Pearson.

The 1988 Vickers strike was more than just an industrial action as it affected the whole town. Here workers attend a mass meeting to hear the options open to them.

A vote is taken at a mass meeting. The strike, over fixed summer holidays, was to prove a long and bitter struggle with no real winners.

The dispute attracted national attention and on 11 July a rally was held through the town streets.

Support came to the Barrow strikers from all over the country and a shop was set up providing bread and other groceries to shipyard families left with little money to survive on.

Long summer weeks on strike also gave opportunities to enjoy some sun on the beaches at Walney.

Many businesses were badly hit by lost trade during the 1988 strike. Here a town fish and chip shop closes until better times return.

The official paperwork involved in processing the financial details of thousands of strikers led to huge queues like this one in Forshaw Street in July 1988.

Everyone in Barrow had an opinion over the rights and wrongs of the strike. This retriever knew whose side he was on.

Barrow's Submariners

Youngsters wave their flags for the launch of *Dreadnought* in October 1960.

The 3,000-ton *Dreadnought* eases out of Barrow docks in 1960.

Shipyard workers on the *Dreadnought* submarine wait for the Duke of Edinburgh to arrive on a visit in June 1959.

Cutting a cake as part of the commissioning ceremony for HMS *Osiris* in January 1964.

A scene inside the galley on HMS *Dreadnought* in January 1963.

The launch of *Osiris* in November 1962.

The main pressure hull frames for *Valiant* on Michaelson Road. The 3,500-ton submarine was launched in December 1963.

The Vickers Oceanic mini-sub *Pisces*.

The submarine *Warspite* under construction in August 1964. The boat was launched in September 1965.

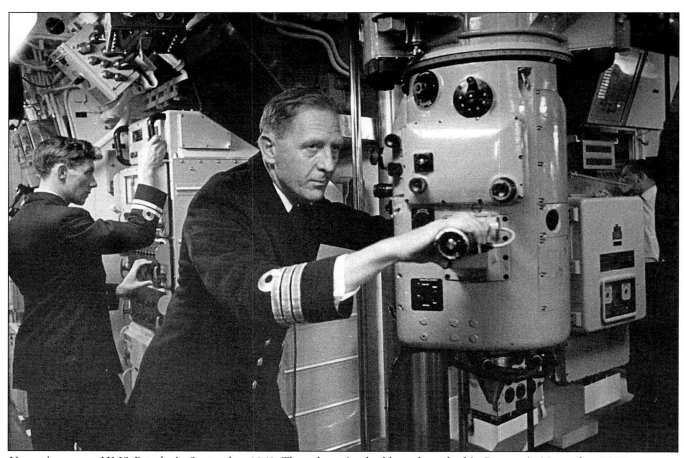

Up periscope on HMS *Repulse* in September 1968. The submarine had been launched in Barrow in November 1967.

The launch of the 3,500-ton *Courageous* in March 1970.

The champagne bottle is about to be sent crashing into the hull of *Courageous* during the launch ceremony in 1970.

The *Tonelero* goes down the slipway in November 1972. The submarine was built for the Brazilian government.

The 2,030-ton submarine *Riachuelo* was built for Brazil and launched in September 1975.

HMS *Superb* leaving Ramsden Dock in 1976 after the commissioning ceremony. The 4,400-ton submarine had been launched in November 1974.

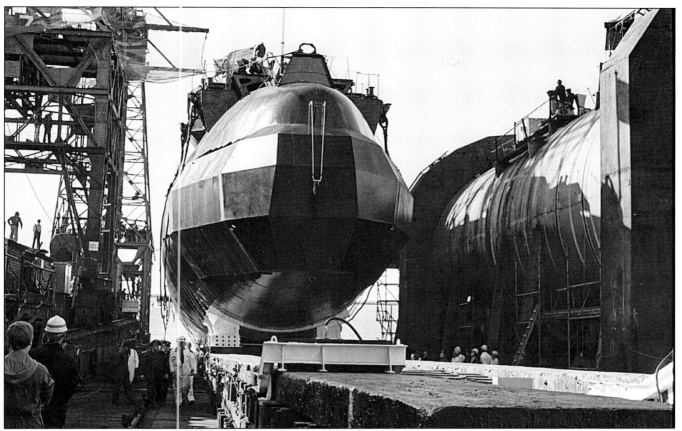

The launch of the 4,400-ton *Splendid* at Barrow in October 1979.

The Princess Royal inspects Marines at the commissioning of HMS *Talent* in 1990. The 4,500-ton submarine had been launched at Barrow in April 1988.

Crowds at the launch ceremony for *Torbay* in March 1985. The submarine was commissioned by the Royal Navy in February 1987.

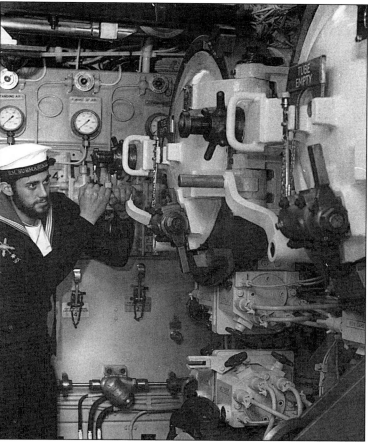

Barrow mayor Irene Lucas takes a tour of an *Oberon* class submarine which was visiting Barrow in 1986.

A view inside the torpedo compartment on HMS *Resolution* during the commissioning ceremony in October 1967.

Swiftsure was launched in September 1971 as the first of a new class of deep diving nuclear-powered hunter-killer submarines.

The submarine *Triumph* at Barrow in 1991.

Upholder at Barrow in 1990. It is due to become part of the Canadian navy.

The Vickers band plays off *Tireless*, launched in March 1984.

Excited youngsters at the launch of the 4,500-ton *Trenchant* in November 1986.

The 4,500-ton *Turbulant* was launched in December 1982 and commissioned in April 1984.

The huge shape of the 15,000-ton *Vanguard* slowly emerging from the Devonshire Dock Hall in 1992.

Sailors on parade for the commissioning of HMS *Vanguard* in August 1993.

Crowds seeking the best vantage points on Walney Channel as *Vanguard* leaves Barrow in 1993.

A large section of *Vigilant* on the move through Barrow Island in December 1990.

Lady Heather Newman with VSEL chief executive Sir Noel Davies at the rolling out ceremony for the second Trident submarine *Victorious* in September 1993.

Victorious edges out of the Devonshire Dock Hall in 1993.

Barrow's Ships

The SS *Stratheden* leaving Barrow for sea trials. The 23,722-ton ship was launched in June 1937.

Oriana was a magnificent sight with all lights blazing as construction work continued day and night at Barrow shipyard.

The luxury liner *Oriana* taking shape on the stocks at Barrow.

The *Oriana* was the height of cruising style and elegance and remains one of Barrow's best-loved ships. The 41,923-ton ship was launched at Barrow in September 1957.

You get an idea of the scale of the *Oriana* as it towers over the buildings of St George's Square on the left of this 1960 photograph. The liner was built for the Orient Steam Navigation Company.

The launch of the 27,632-ton liner *Oronsay* in May 1950.

Putting the name on the boiler casing of the 28,396-ton Orient liner *Orcades*. The liner was launched in October 1947 and was scrapped in 1973.

Chusan was the biggest liner completed in the world during 1950. It weighed in at 24,261 tons and was 672 feet long. It could carry 1,500 passengers and crew at 22 knots.

The first-class lounge on the port side on the Barrow liner *Chusan* in 1950.

The newly-launched liner *Chusan* leaving Barrow in 1949.

The Empress of Russia on fire in Buccleuch Dock in 1945. It was towed to Ward's scrapyard in Barrow in 1946.

Danish liner *Copenhagen* at Barrow in 1974. It later became the Russia-owned *Oaecca*.

The Danish liner *Prins Hendricks* was built in Barrow in 1974.

Taking the strain on the 100,000-ton BP tanker *British Admiral* in 1965.

The tanker *British Glory* was the fourth built at Barrow for the British Tanker Company. It weighed 36,000 tons. It was launched in February 1957.

British Admiral was the first 100,000-ton tanker built in Europe. It took crude oil from the Middle East to BP's Angle Bay Ocean Terminal at Pembrokeshire.

The 20,300-ton bulk carrier *Methane Princess* under construction at Barrow. It was launched in June 1963.

The launch of the 2,700-ton *Almirante Rivero*s for the Chilean navy in December 1958.

The 23,000-ton aircraft carrier *Hermes* at Barrow in 1959. It was launched in February 1953.

Work under way on *Sheffield* in 1970. It was hit and set on fire during the Falklands War in 1982.

The Queen launches *Sheffield* on 10 May 1971.

Crowds watch the 3,500-ton *Cardiff* leaving the slipway at Barrow in February 1974.

The launch ceremony for *Cardiff* in 1974.

The handing over ceremony for *Hercules* in 1976. It had been ordered by the Argentine government and launched in October 1972.

HMS *Manchester* before the launch in November 1980.

The giant 16,000-ton carrier *Invincible* in 1977.

Few sights were more impressive in 1970s Barrow than the huge shell of *Invincible* slowing taking shape.

Royal Marines on duty for the commissioning of the frigate HMS *Mohawk* in 1963.

The 2,300-ton tribal class frigate *Mohawk* was launched in May 1962.

Aircraft carrier *Ocean* in Buccleuch Dock in 1997.

The *Bay Fisher* in 1958, part of the Barrow fleet of James Fisher and Sons.

A 45-ton nuclear fuel flask being unloaded from the *Stream Fisher* in 1969.

The 3,325-ton Brazilian navy training ship *Almirante Saldanha* was launched from Barrow in December 1933.

The schooner *Emily Barratt* at Barrow in 1989. It was eventually broken up at Barrow Dock Museum.

Training ship *Royalist* visiting Barrow docks in 1991.

Mark Harvey demonstrates to Kayleigh Jacques how to steer a ship on board HMS *Walney* in 1997.

The Barrow-built HMS *Manxman* in May 1964.

The pulp boat *Thora Dan* unloading at Barrow in 1973.

Greek cargo ship *Spyros Niarchos* is manoeuvred by tugs in Buccleuch Dock.

The 20,889-ton *San Gregorio* was launched at Barrow in July 1957 for the Eagle Oil and Shipping Company.

The Barrow lifeboat gets a touch of paint in the 1950s.